How to Solve a Rubik's Cube

The Easy Solution to The Rubik's Cube, A Beginner's Guide to Solving This Puzzle, Quick and Easily

Chad Bomberger

Legal & Disclaimer

The information contained in this book and its contents is not designed to replace or take the place of any form of medical or professional advice; and is not meant to replace the need for independent medical, financial, legal or other professional advice or services, as may be required. The content and information in this book has been provided for educational and entertainment purposes only.

The content and information contained in this book has been compiled from sources deemed reliable, and it is accurate to the best of the Author's knowledge, information, and belief. However, the Author cannot guarantee its accuracy and validity and cannot be held liable for any errors and/or omissions. Further, changes are periodically made to this book as and when needed. Where appropriate and/or necessary, you must consult a professional (including but not limited to your doctor, attorney, financial advisor or such other professional advisor) before using any of the suggested remedies, techniques, or information in this book.

Upon using the contents and information contained in this book, you agree to hold harmless the Author from and against any damages, costs, and expenses, including any legal fees potentially resulting from the application of any of the information provided by this book. This disclaimer applies to any loss, damages or injury caused by the use and application, whether directly or indirectly, of any advice or information presented, whether for breach of contract, tort, negligence, personal injury, criminal intent, or under any other cause of action.

You agree to accept all risks of using the information presented in this book.

You agree that by continuing to read this book, where appropriate and/or necessary, you shall consult a professional (including but not limited to your doctor, attorney, or financial advisor or such other advisor as needed) before using any of the suggested remedies, techniques, or information in this book.

Table of Contents

Chapter 1: Introduction 1

Chapter 2: Understanding the Rubik's Cube Puzzle......................3

    A Short History of Rubik's Cube..4

    Well-known Personalities Associated with Rubik's Cube 6

    Rubik's Cube Associations..6

Chapter 3: Getting Started 7

    Why Solve Rubik's Cube? 7

    How Do You Get Started? 8

    The Structure of the Cube 9

    Terminology..10

    Naming the Pieces...10

    The Faces...12

Chapter 4: Layer By Layer Solution 17

    Solving the Upper Face (1st Layer)..17

    The Middle Layer 25

    Yellow Face: The Completion...28

Conclusion...42

Chapter 1

Introduction

If you have been searching for ways to solve Rubik's cube, you must have come across and even tried different methods available online. Well, if none has worked so far, you are reading the right book. In this EBook, we are going to discuss in details different methods that can help you solve Rubik's cube with the least steps possible. We are going to expose you to different approaches, each of them explained in details, so that you have the feel, practice and choose what suits you the most.

The book is short and precise to the point. With very easy language and few but clear algorithms, our target is to make sure that you get to success before you get bored. It is for this reason that we focused on an easy step by step procedure. If you are a beginner, this was written for you. We have clear diagrams to guide every move you make and explain all possible scenarios.

There are hundreds and perhaps thousands of eBook online, but all you need is something that gives you quick results. With this book, you will be able to solve your cube in less than 30 minutes and memorize the steps in a matter of hours. Nothing stops you from becoming a professional in a week or less.

What to Expect from the Beginners Methods

In this particular method, we are going to share; there are only a few algorithms you have to memorize, making it very suitable for the beginners. With a high level of efficiency, you should be able to solve the Rubik's cube within 60 or fewer seconds. I have seen my friends solve it in the 30s with the method we are going to describe. However, if you can't do it in the 30s, don't be discouraged. Personally, I have not achieved that speed yet. However, if you try and it works out in

30s seconds, you are too advanced for this method, I recommend that you move to the advanced or higher levels.

In addition to easy to understand algorithms, this method also comes with the advantage of being fairly scalable. That means that if you want to upgrade to the intermediate or advanced stage, you simply scale this method by adding other algorithms. Similarly, it can be developed to an expert stage in the same way. To make your work easier, we accompany the explanations with diagrams for easy demonstration.

Chapter 2
Understanding the Rubik's Cube Puzzle

RUBIK'S cube is ranked in the list of the top puzzles in the world. The cube is designed with a series of mini-cubes of white colors. The challenge is designed to challenge your mind and capture your imagination. It is solved by moving the pieces of different colors. Every time it is crumbled, you have to solve it by matching all cubes of one particular color on one face. If you make to have 'yellow' or 'white' or any other color on one face, you have just solved the puzzle. With the amazing movement of colors and pieces, each cube puzzle offers an intricate challenge that is always hard to put down.

Solving a Rubik's Cube is always challenging and ever fulfilling. Once you master the art, it quickly turns into a hobby. I soon gain experience and start learning the tips and tricks you quickly become a master in the game and solve the puzzle very quickly. Soon, it will not be just about solving the cube but solving it while being timed. That is speed cubing. For true professionals, it goes beyond just speed cubing; their pleasure comes from solving the cube blindfolded and timed. It that surprising? It could be you.

It is estimated that most of the children all over the world would know and have played with a Rubik's Cube, with the other name magic cube. Indeed, when we were young, the Rubik's cube is considered as the educational toys which can be used to develop children's intelligence. The children who can quickly recover the previous disorder Rubik's cube always considered as the popular child prodigy. In fact, the Rubik's cube is not only the kid's toys but also the remarkable invention. Along with Klotski invented in China and Solitaire invented in the France, they are the three incredible games in the intelligence community. Believe it or not, Rubik's cube is listed as the top 100 inventions of the 20th century, all of which have the most influential impact. It is not the evaluation only by the Rubik's cube enthusiasts, but the sociologists' viewpoint according to the Rubik's cube's influence and role on the human development.

A Short History of Rubik's Cube

Now that you are desired to pursue your desire and become a Rubik's cube master, it is only fair that you get to understand how this puzzle became one of the most popular puzzles today. The history behind the Rubik's cube does not stretch as long as you may imagine. It was invented back in 1974 by Erno Rubik, a Hungarian sculptor, and Professor of Architecture. But that is the 3x3x3 cube, before that, Larry Nichols invented the 2x2x2 in March 1970. It was famous as a 'Puzzle with Pieces Rotatable in Groups.' He immediately filed a Canadian patent for his innovation. At the time, the cube invented by Nichols relied on a magnet to hold the mini-cubes together. He succeeded to get a U. S. Patent number 3, 655, 2001 on April 11, 1972. This was two years before the Rubik invented his 3x3x3 cube.

The first Rubik's cube (3x3x3 cube) was originally invented by Rubik, the Professor of Architecture from the Hungarian, in 1974. In the beginning, he wanted to use this as the training tools for his students. What is a pity, he found that he could not recover the original shape after rotating for a few steps optionally. Then he spent several weeks in studying the relationship of the every piece of the magic cube, and finally, he succeeds. In his viewpoint, it is the great educational things which could be used to develop intelligence. Therefore he wrote a detailed description of this toy. In 1977, the first batch of Rubik's cube goods appeared in Hungary and in 1978, during the International Congress of Mathematicians held in the Helsinki, the capital of Finland, the Hungarian mathematician introduced the magic cube to all the participating experts and scholars, which aroused great attention. Subsequently, the first Rubik's cube theory, the research group was established in the UK and David Singmaster, one of the mathematician, was known as the Rubik's Cube master.

In the 1980s, the Rubik's Cube trend has reached the first peak, and at that time, it is known as the most educational toys up to now. Because of the in depth research on the Rubik's cube, more and more people, not only the children, are more likely to play with the Rubik's cube. In addition to the exercise of thinking ability and the brain's activities, finger sensitivity can also be developed from the playing process, which cannot be replaced by other sports or toys.

As I have already alluded, there are actually many different approaches to solving Rubik's cube. For simplicity, these approaches can be divided into two main categories. These are:

In this book, you may not get all you want, but if you are a newbie, I bet you will find something to take home with you. I must add that for intermediate, advanced and expert players; there are great websites, videos and other online materials that might be of great help. The few methods we have discussed in this book will be complimented with other materials we will be sharing later on.

I understand that most of the materials that you might have read by now may not provide the solution you are looking for. The reason is simple, although many documents have nice titles targeting newbies, the methods discussed are either for intermediate or advanced 'cubers.' It is for this reason I write this EBook. This is not to say that this is the best that you can ever find, but it will be very helpful in your quest to improve your skills. We have tried these methods with many of my students with a lot of success, and that is why I am so confident you will find them useful.

Well-known Personalities Associated with Rubik's Cube

Well, millions of people solve Rubik's puzzle every day all over the world, but a few people have made their names solving the Rubik's cubes. These are the people who compete in major tournaments organized in different cities all over the world. If Rubik's Cube has its own version of the hall of fame, then you will be sure to find some of the names such as Lucas Etter, Rami Sbahi, Kevin Hays, and Minh Thai just to mention a few.

Rubik's Cube Associations

After learning the basics, take your time to familiarize yourself with the Rubik's Cube professional bodies around you. There are several benefits that come with associations and professional bodies dedicated to developing Rubik's cube. Get one near you and become a member. You are sure to meet experienced people, gain insights and useful ideas and make friends that are like-minded and share the same passion with you. If you are interested in competitions and developing your skills to become a professional, then these bodies are the best place to be. The professional bodies will put you in touch with the boards and committees organizing tournaments and make sure you get to compete. The World Cube Association is a major association that you should consider. However, start by finding the associations within your locality.

Chapter 3
Getting Started

Why Solve Rubik's Cube?

I still remember my first ever interaction with the Rubik's cube with lots of pleasure. I was still a young boy back then. My father comes with this multicolored toy. He explained that if I learn to solve it very first, I could score better grades at school. This was exciting, I was not particularly scoring good grades, and anything that could make my mom proud of me was a welcome idea.

Then it all started, the challenge was solving the Rubik's cube. Unfortunately, some days passed, weeks and months, all my attempts were in vain. My father did not get tired explaining and encouraging me, but I was losing interest very fast. Then one day, as if by divine intervention, I solved it. I still remember that day, it was a rainy day, I took the cube, smiled and mentioned to myself:" Okay, I'm heading to clear up the cube as my father explained to me." And so, as a pretty persistent human being, I spent the entire afternoon hoping to clear up the challenge, and every time just did not perform. All those who have an understanding of what I am declaring plainly know how much aggravation carries the resolving of this nonsense. And so day after day I tried using and failed every single time. Soon after two weeks, I did it! I was content as I won the lottery. He smiled and explained attempt do it once again. I imagined: "Okay, no difficulty, I'll do it once again." Immediately after many attempts, I failed once again, once again and all over again. I assumed: "Dear God, is it possible? I will certainly not figure out." My father just smiled.

Right after months fixing this puzzle, I realized just how excellent it is, how substantially creativeness was invested in its building and of the program I discovered how to fix Rubik's cube problem. And at the end of this tale, I can tell that persistence is superior, but without expertise, it is not worthy of consideration. If you want to find out how to remedy Rubik's cube challenge, continue reading.

Rubik's has been rated as a very pleasurable yet very difficult game. This explains why not so many people carry the cube around with them in the public buses and trains. It's difficult to solve. We can struggle for hours, days and sometimes even weeks, but once we solve it, we get a sense of pride and satisfaction.

How Do You Get Started?

Dedication and commitment are all that matters.

You should approach solving Rubik's cube as a regular activity and not a one-time achievement. Take is as a pastime activity. Something you consider for your leisure activity. You can only gather the necessary knowledge and skills if you are able to engage in Rubik's regularly. Well, this is not to say that it should take precedence over other important activities, but consider it whenever free. If you find yourself idle in the back of the taxi or maybe you are on the train/plane traveling from one city to the other, solve your cube before you find yourself dozing off.

The majority of people takes Rubik's as a hobby, but a few take it to the next level. These are the people who solve Rubik's cube for monetary reward or some other forms of reward. These are the 'professionals.' As an 'amateur' the target is to learn as much as you can before settling into one of the two categories. The 'hobbyists' and 'amateurs' don't receive any form of compensation for the professionals who are timed and compete for compensation.

Assuming you take it as a hobby, that does not give you license to be lazy. You never know, very soon you will find yourself in the company of friends or work colleagues in team building activities and solve Rubik's cube is one of the activities with points for your team. If you cannot step up on behalf of your colleagues and earn them points, then your knowledge is useless at the time. Ideally, once you choose it as a hobby, get committed, find other people who enjoy solving Rubik's cube and challenge them to compete, even if not for money. By engaging with other players, you get to improve in speed and tactics. Taking the Rubik's cube as a hobby is one thing, but succeeding in it is a completely different thing. It is for this reason that it is advisable to take your new hobby seriously.

The Structure of the Cube

Mathematically, we all agree that that $3x3x3=27$. So, if you are asked the number of little cubes that make one complete Rubik's cube, you quickly rush to the solution as 27. This is true, however, instead of retaining the image of 27 little 'cubies' in your mind, have a picture of it as an object with 6 fixed centers or faces. The centers are 'fixed' but should be able to rotate on their own axis. In addition to the six centers, the object you are looking at has 8 corners and 12 edges. The corners and edges get to rotate around the object. That is the picture you should have in your mind as we begin.

Well, the centers are fixed (at least in your mind), so use the center color to define the color for that particular face. If you remember what we have discussed so far, you will be able to avert many problems that might arise along the way. The cost of not having the picture I have described is a waste of time trying steps that are not logical. Imagine having 8 of the 9 cubies in what appears to be the right position, and you soon start scratching your head trying to picture how to put the corner piece in an edge position. Well, if the center is white, it does not matter even if you have 8 of 9 blue cubies on the right position, this is simply a white face, and you will be wasting time with mechanically impossible moves.

Terminology

Before we move any further, it is best to first get the basics. These are the terminologies. When I say F, what do I mean? We are going to describe the solutions for the 2nd and 3rd layers. From now on, we will adopt the standard cube notations for further references. So let's get to it straight away.

Naming the Pieces

Center Pieces

Center pieces are located at the center of each of the six faces. There are only six in total and each is surrounded by eight pieces. They are unique in that they have one side (face visible) and do not move.

Corner Piece

Corner pieces are located on each face. Each have three visible sides and each side makes up one part of a face.

Edge Pieces

The edge pieces are located in between two corner pieces. Each has two visible sides.

We are going to name the faces after letters, with the first letter of the face representing that face. There are 6 faces, and therefore we have six letters in capital for this purpose. Let's have a look.

The Faces

1. F=front face

2. B=back face

3. R=right face

4. L=left face

5. U=up face

6. D=down face

For clarity, the moves are accompanied with an apostrophe or simply the number two (2). So, we have either F, F', or F2. So, what do we mean by each of these?

- A letter not accompanied by anything else is used to show 90 degrees clockwise turn (e.g. R).

- A letter with an apostrophe is used to show a 90 degrees anti-clockwise turn (e.g. R').

- A letter accompanied with numerical number 2 is to show that the turn is facing 180 degrees in any direction (e.g. F2).

- Understanding the Movements

- In order to understand the Rubik's Cube movements, we assume that you are **directly looking at the face you are working on**. There are two specific movements; these are the clockwise movement and the anticlockwise movements. These movements are indicated using the letters used to denote the face. For example, a clockwise movement of the upper face is shown as **U** while the anticlockwise for the same face is shown as **U'**

U': Rotate the upper face 90 degrees counter clockwise

U: Rotate the upper face 90 degrees clockwise

Use of number **2**: Number '**2**' is added after the instruction as an indication that the move has to be repeated. If added after **F**, the instruction reads **F2**. This is to say 'rotate the front face **(F)** clockwise twice or 180 degrees.

So, what does R U'L2 Mean?

From what we have just discussed, it is actually easy. R U'L2 simply stands for the following steps:

First, turn the right (R) face 90 degrees in the clockwise direction;

Turn the upper (U) face 90 degrees in the anticlockwise direction;

Turn the left (L) face 180 degrees

So, how do you determine whether it should go clockwise or anti-clockwise? This is determined by yourself. **Look directly at a particular face you want to turn and determine the clockwise direction from that position.**

However, we make a very important assumption for all the algorithms. The assumption is that the core of the cube will remain fixed all the way as you make different movements. With each algorithm, the faces simply turn around a fixed core. Well, this is to say that you have to learn how to position your cube before starting the algorithms.

Chapter 4
Layer By Layer Solution

Solving the Upper Face (1st Layer)

To start off, turn your cube so that the WHITE center piece is on the U face. This is easy, just check around and until you locate a face with the white face already at the center. This becomes your U face. Use this face as a reference point when talking about the other faces like the front (**F**), back (**B**), down (**D**), right (**R**) and left (**L**). Note, you will be holding the cube in its current position (the **U** face looking at the roof) until instructed otherwise.

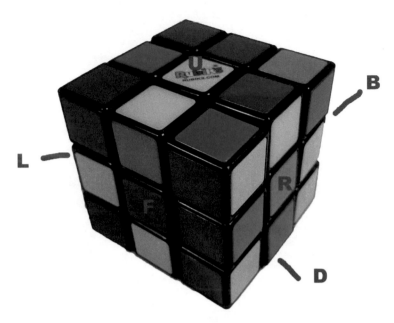

The target of the initial movements we are going to make is to bring the white edge cubies around the white center cubie. By the end, there should be a formation of a white cross on the U face. Also, remember that we are using a standard Rubik's Cube. This cube has the white face directly opposite the yellow face. The instructions are not straight forward for the older versions of Rubik's Cube in which the white face is not necessarily opposite the yellow one.

Note: The white center cubie should not be moved from the U face. It is the most common mistake at this stage.

Step 1: Make sure the white center cubie is on the U face

Step 2: Form a white cross on the U face by moving the white edge cubies to the upper face. This can be completed using different techniques, and we don't need an algorithm. Try the following movements:

- **White edge square sitting at the bottom L or R row**: rotate the L or R row once. This pushes the white square to the 2nd (middle) row. See next move.

- **White edge square sitting in the middle (2nd) L or R row**: Rotate the face next to the white square. This could be either B or F face. Continue rotating until the white square moves to the D face.

- **White edge square sitting at the Down (D) face**: Rotate the D face to move the white square opposite a non-white edge piece at the U face. Looking at the upper or (U) face, the non-white cubies are considered the empty spaces. Turn your cube in such a way that the targeted 'empty space' is now located at the U face but next to the F face (i.e UF). Next, complete an F2 move. This involves turning the front face a total of 180 degree (90 degrees twice). This moves the white square to the right Upper-Front position.

- Repeat the steps for the remaining white edge squares to bring all to the upper face.

Step 3: Extending the Cross to Corners

Take a look at the cube you are holding with the U face at its right position. Look at the edge pieces on the remaining faces; these are the F, B, L, and R faces. The target is to create a cross in each of these faces. The cross should match the color of the edge piece. It starts by matching the center piece with the edge piece that borders the U face i.e. if the edge piece of R face bordering U face is yellow, then make the center square piece also yellow. To accomplish these for the four faces, follow the steps below:

Match the upper edge of at least two of the four faces with the center square of the same color. You can achieve this by simply rotating the U face while checking. If you are lucky enough to have the four faces matching, just skip the rest of the steps.

Turn the cube (don't rotate) to bring one of the unmatched faces to R. Remember to retain the position of white face as U.

Perform an F2 rotation move to bring one of the white edges to D (down) face. Determine the corresponding color of the same (white edge at D face) piece. In our case it's red.

Rotate the D face to bring the red edge square beneath the red center piece.

Now perform R2 rotation (remember R2 is now also the red face, rotate it 180 degrees). This returns the white face to its original U position. By now, the upper edge piece and the center piece should now be matching for R, B, L and F faces.

Step4: Bringing the White Corners to the Right Position at the White Face

Remember, your white face now has the cross made of white center and edge pieces. The objective is now to bring the white corners to complete the white face. However, it is not straightforward like other earlier steps; you, therefore, need to pay closer attention to these steps:

Check the D face to locate a corner piece with a WHITE part on it. Remember that corner pieces have 3 sides each with a unique color. When checking for a white corner from the D face, remember that the specific white face of the corner cubie may not be necessarily on the D face, but that part of that corner is on the D face. For clarity, let's name the corner piece with white face and two other colors for the two sides as white/X/Y.

Now that you have seen the location of the white/X/Y piece on the D face, the next task is to rotate the D face in such a way that brings the white/X/Y between the face with X color as its center cubie and the face with Y as its center cubie. These 'X' and 'Y' faces could be L, R, F, or B faces.

Next, turn the cube to put the *white/X/Y* piece we are focusing on to the down-right-front position. Don't mind of the position of the particular colors of this cubie though. Take a close look, and you will see that the color of the center cubie of the front and the right faces match the colors X and Y. At this point, the top or Upper (U) face is still white.

This leaves us with the following 3 scenarios and solutions:

- White square cubie on the F face; apply **FDF'** algorithm

Orange

- White square cubie on the R face; apply the **R'D'R** algorithm to orient it

BLUE

- White square cubie on the D face; apply the **FD2F'D'FDF'** algorithm

WHITE

Repeat the steps with the remaining Corners

The next few steps are about repeating the steps above. At the end of it, you still have the U face completely white with the upper row squares of F, R, L and B faces have a color that matches the respective center cubies.

If it happens that your cubie has its white corner on the U face but not in the right position. You need to relocate it to the right position. You will notice that the white corner is in the wrong position if it is on the white face (U face) but the colors of X, and Y are not matching the center piece. If this is the case, simply turn your cube to have it on an Upper-Front-Right position. At this position, apply the FDF' algorithm. This directly brings the white square to the D face. Apply the steps the earlier stage to get it to the right position.

The Middle Layer

Step 1: Inspect the D face for any edge cubie without any yellow in it: Remember, your upper face is now white and the down face is yellow though incomplete. Note the colors of that particular edge cubie.

Let's say the one color is X and the second color of the same piece is Y, remember we are dealing with edge piece that has only two visible sides and not a corner piece that has 3 visible sides.

Step 2: Bring the face with the color X to the front by simply turning the cube. When turning the cube, retain the U face at its position (upper). This is more of a simple spin of the cube as a whole. When complete, X center piece is now part of the new F (front) face.

Step 3: Aligning the D face: This is done by rotating the D in any direction you choose. The target is to bring the X/Y edge cubie to the down-back or DB position. Check to confirm that the color X on the cubie is on the D face and the color Y of the same edge cubie is on the B face.

Step 4: Use color Y to adjust the cube: The target is to adjust the cube, but the right move depends on the location of the Y center cubie. Consider the following possibilities:

- Color Y center matching the R face center piece: use the **FDF'D'R'D'R**.

- Color Y center matching the L face center piece: use the **F'D'FD LDL'**.

Step 5: The procedure in step four is repeated to complete the top two layers, i.e., from the D face, get an edge piece that has no yellow squares on it. However, proceed to next step if none is available. Basically, apply the logarithms described in step four, and by the time you are done, you will note that the middle and top rows of the front (F), the back (B), left (L), and right (R) faces matches.

In the event that you have a cubie that is in the proper location, but the colors are flipped. Proceed with the following method to switch it. This is a lengthy one, so be careful not to make a mistake, it could be hard to revert back to how you had it.

How to Adjust for the wrong orientation:

Use the following algorithm

L D' L' D' F' D F D2 D L D' L' D' F' D F

Step 6: Need for adjustments should all the D edge cubies include yellow. Take a second look at the edge pieces of your D face. Of the four edge pieces, each piece has two colors, one on the D face and the other lying on the corresponding face depending on its position on the cube. None of the colors of any of these edge pieces should be yellow as long as that edge cubie has one side on the D face.

Yellow Face: The Completion

Step 1: Turn your cube to bring the yellow center face to upper (U) position. From now on, your U faces changes from the white face to the yellow face. The cube remains in this position for the rest of the steps until all the faces are solved.

Step 2: Creating a cross sign on the yellow or new U face. First, inspect and take note of the yellow edge cubies already on the U face. Don't confuse the corner (3-faced cubies) with the edge (2-faced cubies). After inspecting the number of yellow edge pieces on the U face, we are left with four possible scenarios and solutions.

Scenario 1: <u>2 yellow edge cubies opposite each other on the U face</u>. Rotate the U face to position the two edges on the upper-left and upper-right positions. Next, apply the algorithm **BLUL'U'B'**

Scenario 2: <u>2 adjacent yellow cubies on the upper-front and upper-right positions</u> forming an arrow that points back left: Simply apply the algorithm **BULU'L'B'**.

Scenario 3: <u>No Yellow Edge Cubie on the U face</u>: In such cases, apply either of the algorithms described in scenario 1 and 2. The either of the algorithms will bring 2 yellow edge cubies to the U face. Inspect their position and apply scenario 1 or 2 algorithms depending on their position.

Scenario 4: <u>Four Edges already present on the U face</u>: If this is the case, move to the next step.

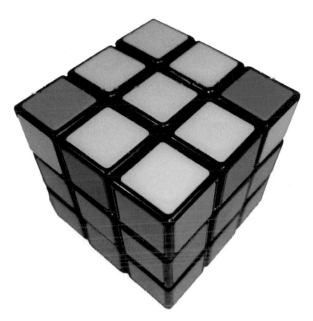

Step 3: Now that we have the cross we want to line up two of the top row middle cubies with the center pieces of the F, B, R or L faces. There are three possible scenarios

Scenario 1: They are adjacent to each other. Hold the cube so that one of the solved sides is on the right face and the other solved side is in the back face. Proceed to algorithm.

Scenario 2: They are across from each other. Hold the cube so that one of the solved sides is in the front and one of the solved sides is in the back. Proceed to algorithm.

Scenario 3: All four sides line up. Proceed to next step.

Algorithm: **R U R' U R U2 R' U**

After completing this algorithm, all of the middle cubies in the top row will now line up with the center cubies on the F, B, R, and L faces.

Step 4: Now that they are lining up, you want to look for a corner cube that is solved correctly, such that it matches all adjacent sides. If you find a cube that is in the correct corner, rotate the cube such that this corner is on the top right of the Front face. Proceed to the algorithm. If there are no matching corners, proceed to the algorithm.

Correct Corner, don't worry about orientation yet

Continue with this algorithm until all 4 corners are in the correct locations. Such that, the corners are in the right corners (this means that the corner cube colors match up with all adjacent colors, the corner cube does not have to be in the correct orientation at this point.)

Algorithm: U R U' L' U R' U' L

Once all of the corner cubes are in the correct corners, proceed to the next step.

Step 5: Now that all of the corners are in the correct corners. We want to fix the orientation so that the yellow is on the U face and the corresponding colors match the correct faces.

Rotate the cube such that an incorrectly oriented corner is on the top right of the cube and proceed with the following algorithm.

Algorithm: **R'DRD'**

– repeat this algorithm until the corner you are trying to solve for is correctly oriented (This may take several times) Now when you complete this, the rest of the cube will look unsolved. Do not worry, this will solve itself. Now turn the U face 90 degrees clockwise until the next unsolved corner is in the upper left of the cube. Repeat the above algorithm (**R'DRD'**) until this next one is solved. Continue this process until all corners are solved

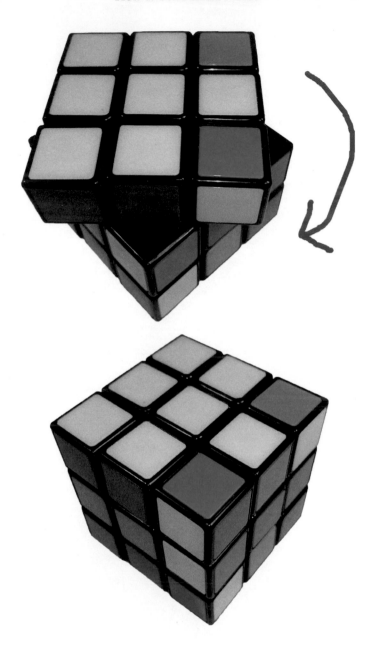

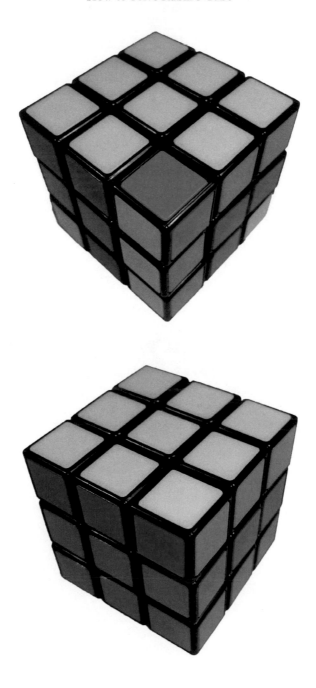

Now just rotate the cube until all the rows line up and then you will have successfully completed you rubik's cube! Congratulations!

Conclusion

The solution I have shared should get you started, just practice a few times and you will be good to go! It is my pleasure to make you a professional. Once you are done with the beginner's method, you can try more advance methods from the intermediate to professional levels.

Finally, I wish to thank you for downloading this eBook. Please feel free to share your experiences, challenges and concerns. Your comments will help us improve the book.

I hope you have enjoyed this book as much as I've enjoyed writing it! If you would please take 5 minutes of your time to review this book, it would mean so much to me to hear how you've enjoyed it!

Amazon.com

85079688R00027

Made in the USA
Lexington, KY
28 March 2018